D0529101

Selling Successfully Online
Over 120 Top Tips for Running an Ecommerce Web Site

Chris Barling & Bruce Townsend

Actinic

Selling Successfully Online
Over 120 Top Tips for Running an Ecommerce Web Site
By Chris Barling & Bruce Townsend

Copyright (c) Actinic Software Ltd, Globe House, Lavender Park Road,
West Byfleet, Surrey KT14 6ND.
All rights reserved. Printed in the United Kingdom.

January 2008: Second edition.

Published by Actinic Software Ltd.

While every precaution has been taken in the preparation of this book,
the authors and the publisher assume no responsibility for errors and
omissions, or for damages resulting from the use of information
contained herein.

Actinic, Actinic Catalog, Actinic Express, Actinic Designer and
Actinic Business are registered trademarks of Actinic Software Ltd.

ISBN 0-9550688-0-0

Contents

Introduction

In a remarkably short space of time, the internet has moved from being a new and relatively unknown technology to being an accepted part of everyday life. In recent years it has been the fastest growing sales channel in most sectors of business. Not long ago companies asked the question, 'Can we afford to start selling online?' Now they are asking, 'Can we afford not to?'

Since 1996, Actinic has specialized in helping small and medium businesses to sell on the internet, and tens of thousands of businesses have got started with Actinic.

Actinic also supplies EPOS and mail order systems for small and medium companies, which gives us valuable insights into ecommerce in an overall business context.

In this guide we share the basic steps to setting up shop on the web, together with the key lessons we have learned that can make the difference between success and failure. (For more information about Actinic products, see the last page of this publication).

We've organized the document as a series of tips under different headings, so that it's easy to dip in and out of particular topics. We hope that you find this format helpful.

Introduction to selling online

Introduction to selling online:

Steps for setting up an online store

TOP TIP **1** First, get informed

The more you know, the better decisions you will make. So look out for articles about ecommerce in the press, attend a trade show or two, and talk to people who are selling online already. Search on Google for related themes such as 'ecommerce' and 'shopping carts', find some informative web sites, and read up about the subject.

TOP TIP **2** Make sure that ecommerce is right for you

If you are selling goods that customers do not need to touch, taste or smell before buying, at a fixed price, then the web is the place to be - especially if your products are hard for customers to find by conventional means. The web can offer your customers the convenience of being able to shop when it suits them, without having to travel or queue. And it offers a level of automation that can help drive down your costs, so you can offer keen prices into the bargain. You can check out the competition by looking on Google for some of the products that you plan to sell.

TOP TIP **3** Get your offering right

Think about why people would want to buy from you. You need to provide them with something which they believe offers more value than the amount they pay, and which you can supply for less than you charge. It's as simple (and difficult) as that.

TOP TIP **4** Keep control of the cost

The less you spend on technology, the more you can afford to spend on promoting your site and bringing in customers. So look ideally for a solution that is low cost and can do what you want to begin with, but offers an upgrade path for the future.

TOP TIP **5** Use technology that already works

Use technology that works, not stuff that's a masterpiece in progress. Why bother debugging software from some start-up, when you could be using an application that is already working on thousands of online stores?

TOP TIP **6** Find a reliable host

Your online store will be able to take orders 24 hours a day - but only so long as it is accessible. You will need a third party to provide the internet space for it. This can be your internet service provider, your ecommerce provider, or a specialized hosting company. Either way, choose one that is reliable. Get a personal recommendation from someone you know, check out one of the regular magazine reviews, or talk to your ecommerce provider.

TOP TIP 7 Make sure you have ownership of your site

Solutions that are rented from a third party and hosted on their server can seem attractive for their low start-up cost and simplicity of use. But they leave you a hostage to the supplier. If the supplier does not provide good service - or worse, goes bust - you will be left high and dry. So choose a solution that covers these eventualities. For instance, you should end up with a full backup on your own PC, which allows you to move your site elsewhere if necessary. Alternatively, your supplier might have a backup partner who can take over in case of problems.

TOP TIP 8 Make security a priority

Both you and your customers need to feel confident that you have adequate protection against hacking and fraud. Choose an ecommerce solution that provides full Payment Card Industry Data Security Standard (PCIDSS) compliance. There's more advice on this later.

TOP TIP 9 Choose an appropriate payment solution

In virtually every market, it's vital to be able to take card payments. In order to do this, you normally need a merchant account which is granted by a "credit card acquirer". All the major banks provide this service. You also need a payment service from someone like WorldPay or Actinic, which will securely handle the transfer of funds from the customer's bank account to your own. However, if you are a start up business it's hard to get your own merchant account, so you may be better off using a service like Paypal. Your shopping cart should be able to support these and a full range of other payment options.

TOP TIP 10 Do it yourself - or not?

The decision whether to go it alone or bring in a professional will depend on a variety of issues. These include your budget; your level of technical knowledge and familiarity with the internet; the amount of customisation you require; the amount of time you have available; and whether you enjoy playing with computers. An ecommerce package can enable you to deploy a good-looking, fully functional site quickly, and at low cost. A web designer will add a professional finish and enhanced features that can generate confidence and boost sales. Either way, make sure the finished site is easy to use for both you and your customers.

TOP TIP 11 Don't forget the marketing

It is all very well opening your shop on the internet, but you need to think about how customers are going to find you. This is probably the most crucial point so we devote a couple of sections of tips to the whole subject.

Introduction to selling online:

Frequently asked questions about selling on the internet

12 How can you take credit card payments across the net?

There are several ways that merchants can take credit card details securely across the net. The method you choose should follow the Payment Card Industry Data Security Standards (PCI DSS). Not all of them do. Merchants who do not follow this standard risk a heavy fine.

The best method is to process card payments in real time on the internet. Providers offering this service include WorldPay, Actinic, Authorize.Net and many others. You pay an upfront fee and a transaction fee, but they do everything for you. This is generally more cost effective than a bureau service (see below), but requires you to have a merchant account with a bank, which is hard to get when you are a start-up. This method is the most suitable for medium and high volume sites.

Then, some of the payment service providers can provide a 'bureau' type service. If you are unable to acquire your own merchant account, they will transact the funds on your behalf - a useful service for some, but not cheap, and they usually hold onto your money for several weeks. This is often the service which new start-ups must settle for.

The final way to take payments is by Paypal, which is easy to set up and allows both Paypal account holders and people with payment cards to buy from your site.

TOP TIP 13 How should people promote their online webstore?

There are lots of ways that this can be done, but for any business there are two no-brainers. The first is to promote the site to all existing customers. If existing customers don't know about the ability to buy online from you, they will go elsewhere. If they like it, they will probably tell their friends. So 'Order online at' and the web address should be on every piece of literature and advertising that a company produces.

The second is to register with search engines. It may take a little time, but it's free and can produce good results. If you plan to do this yourself, make sure you choose an ecommerce solution that will enable you to 'optimise' your pages for the search engines without needing a lot of technical knowledge. There is more information about this later on.

TOP TIP 14 What are the key things to turn browsers into buyers?

In short, remove the reasons why people might not buy. Make your web site oriented towards sales rather than marketing. When prospects are at the site, the marketing process is complete. So, show them the products immediately - don't hide them behind acres of marketing copy. Provide full terms and conditions - it looks more professional, and it protects you. Give your contact details, including a telephone number. Explain your guarantee and returns policy - a rock solid guarantee goes a long way to persuading people to buy. Finally, explain your security and your privacy policy. Again, all of this is expanded later in the document.

TOP TIP **15** What one thing can impress buyers?

Make the site fast. Use graphics effectively, not for the sake of it. Make sure customers can find what they are looking for with a minimum of mouse clicks. Make the checkout process as easy as possible. Remember you're building a site for shoppers, not art lovers. The key is a professional site where visitors can easily find what they're looking for.

TOP TIP **16** Do I need a bespoke design, or can I use an out of the box solution?

Boxed ecommerce solutions are surprisingly powerful and flexible, and offer significant advantages over bespoke - lower cost, quicker site development, more features and greater long-term security. It is worth finding a web designer who can develop a professional design based around a boxed solution. A completely custom-built site is only a good investment if you have special requirements that an out-of-the-box solution cannot fulfil.

TOP TIP **17** Can I compete with the big boys?

The beauty of the internet is that small businesses can compete effectively - nobody knows the size of your company from a URL. Ensure your site is attractive and professional looking. Make sure that you can fulfil orders very promptly - people expect delivery within a day or two. And look for a niche with plenty of customers but not too much competition.

TOP TIP **18** What security risk does transacting online involve?

Less than people think. In fact, the security risks run by web merchants are similar to those of mail-order companies. Just like them, it is sensible for merchants to put anti-fraud policies in place such as phoning to confirm orders that are a particularly high value or that come from parts of the world more prone to fraud.

TOP TIP **19** How much will it cost to set up
a site for selling on the net

The answer varies according to the sophistication and volume of the
site. Professional ecommerce software is available for under £500 (or around
$800), and you can rent web space capable of running such software for
under £100 (or around $150) per annum. Professional site design will
increase your costs, but you can still expect to pay around £2,000–£3,000
(or about $4,000–$6,000) for an average site. Of course more advanced
sites, and sites with multi-user capability for high volume order processing,
will cost more. Just make sure you leave enough in your budget for
marketing your site. No visitors = no sales.

TOP TIP **20** Should merchants maintain their own sites?

A few companies supplying solutions for selling online still keep all
maintenance of ecommerce sites under their direct control. This means that
if you want to change a price, you have to go through the supplier, potentially
delaying your site updates. While this provides the service provider with a
revenue stream, it isn't best for the merchant. The best way is to have a
means of directly updating your site. Also, it's always worth asking what
protection you have if your supplier goes out of business.

TOP TIP **21** Is ecommerce profitable?

Absolutely yes! Selling online can be done on a small or large budget
equally successfully and there are hundreds of thousands of successful users
to prove it. As with all business expansion, do your research, get advice from
trusted sources, decide what you can afford to spend to test the waters, and
then jump!

Marketing your website

Marketing your website:

Top tips for attracting people to your online store

If your great idea is ever to be profitable, people have to know about it. So creating an online store is not enough on its own - just as getting a business telephone number and expecting it to ring is not realistic. To attract visitors to your web site and convert them to customers you have to market the site. Here are some pointers on how you can persuade prospects to visit your site.

TOP TIP **22** Try and get a web address that makes sense

It's worth spending some time thinking about your web site address (URL). Ideally it will be easy to remember, stand out from the crowd and communicate your message. It should be the same as your company name, or include it; and should preferably start with the letter 'A', so that it comes near the top of alphabetical lists. Finding one that is suitable will take some time and probably a lot of investigation, as many good URLs have already been taken.

TOP TIP **23** Start with your existing marketing.

Put your web site address on your existing brochures, advertising, business cards and company letterhead. Wherever you promote your company name, promote your web address as well.

TOP TIP **24** Major on search engines.

Search engines are the number one source of new web site visitors, so it's worth investing some time in learning about them. That is why the whole next tips section is devoted to the subject.

TOP TIP **25** Use forums and newsgroups.

There are lots of places where people hold discussions online. Some of these forums will be talking about your speciality. For instance, if you sell yachting gear, there are plenty of specialist boating forums. Provided that you participate responsibly and provide genuinely helpful advice, you can get the chance to talk about your company, products and offerings. In fact, done skillfully, people will end up asking you for information on your products and services, and that is really powerful. Just make sure you know the forum terms and conditions of each site and abide by them, to avoid tarnishing your reputation.

TOP TIP **26** Spend carefully.

There are lots of opportunities to advertise online, but many can be a waste of time. Before parting with your cash, you should use the same judgement that you would use when deciding whether to advertise in conventional media. Who will be looking at this medium and are they my target market? Getting your message in front of large numbers isn't the issue. They must be potential customers who are interested in your products.

TOP TIP **27** Ask the question, what's working?

It's a sad fact that when it comes to marketing, the anoraks are in the driving seat. Although being creative is crucial, the way to success is to measure the results and put the next round of money where you got the most results last time. So measure everything you do, and try to find out where all your leads and customers come from. When visitors buy from your site, make sure you post a question there asking how they heard about you, or use technology that tracks this automatically. Google supplies a free online service called Google Analytics to help analyse your traffic.

TOP TIP **28** Find sites that are complementary to yours and offer mutual links.

If you can, find specialist sites that cater for your particular niche, and get them to either link to you or put you in their search results. In return, put a link back to them. This can offer added value to your visitors as well as boosting your traffic - it's a win-win situation. It should give you more traffic through the link, and also raise your listing in the search engines, giving more traffic that way as well. You could also set up your own referral scheme so that the linking site receives a share of the sales that they generate. The downside of this is that you need to buy some software or a service to do this.

TOP TIP **29** Use a commercial referral scheme.

There are also a number of referral schemes run commercially that you can join for a fee, and then pay a reward for clickthroughs or sales. Some sites report that this is their most cost-effective method of acquiring sales, but it will depend on what industry you are in.

TOP TIP **30** Generate PR interest.

One of our customers gets national coverage because they have an interesting story - selling products for left handed people. If you can get the press interested, it's worth a fortune in marketing.

TOP TIP **31** Learn from the success of others.

Keep an eye on your competitors, and on successful sites In other market sectors. Don't just copy them; but do learn from what they are doing, and think about how you can adapt good ideas in appropriate ways. Trawl magazines and ecommerce suppliers' web sites for case studies, and find out what other sites attribute their success to.

TOP TIP **32** Provide some additional value at your site.
Can you come up with material for your site that will attract visitors? We provide free advice on ecommerce and the suitability of businesses for trading online, and other useful content. It's worth trying to do something similar at your site.

TOP TIP **33** Remember existing customers.
Once you are up and running, remember that existing customers are your best customers. Make sure that you encourage them to return by making special offers and letting them know what you are doing at your store.

TOP TIP **34** Use email marketing.
There are now a number of responsible companies offering information and services relating to email marketing. They can supply email lists, advice, and delivery technology. They will ensure that you comply with the law, for instance by only sending marketing emails to companies that have opted in to receive them. With email marketing it is often useful to reward a response - for example by offering a discount or free useful white paper for people that click through.

TOP TIP **35** Show your appreciation
for recommendations.

Ask your customers to recommend you to their friends. You are much more likely to make a sale if recommended by someone trusted. If you get a sale as a result of a recommendation and the volumes make it possible, say thank you personally and send some form of reward - whether it is a small gift or a voucher that can be used at your store.

TOP TIP **36** Market offline.

It's true that all of your prospects are online (if they are not online, they can't buy from your store!) But it's sometimes forgotten that 100% of these prospects also have a life offline. You need to ask whether traditional marketing methods such as direct mail may drive traffic cost-effectively to your site.

Marketing your website:

Top tips for good search engine results

There are two ways of getting people to visit your site from search engines. 'Natural' or 'organic' listings are the results which the search engine itself has determined are most relevant to the search. 'Pay per click' or 'sponsored' listings are advertisements which appear when certain specified words have been searched for. The merchant pays each time a searcher clicks on an advert. The good news is that everyone who comes to your site by either method is probably searching for the stuff that you sell.

Eighty percent of users do not look beyond the first page of search engine results. That means if your site is not on the first page, you will hardly be noticed. So make sure at least one page on your site - preferably your home page - is set up as described here, to give yourself the best possible chance of getting noticed.

TOP TIP **37** Choose two or three key phrases that you think customers will use to search for a product or service like yours.

Avoid single words like 'shoes' or very broad terms like 'ironmongery'. There will be so many sites in these kinds of category that you will be very unlikely to get ranked on the first or second pages. Don't try to cover too many phrases on a single page. If you need to target more phrases, set up another page.

TOP TIP 38 Test the phrases you choose.

Use a keyword research tool such as Wordtracker (http://freekeywords.wordtracker.com) to check how many people are actually searching for the phrases you selected. Search the newsgroups for these terms, and see what alternative phrases are used there to describe the same thing. These steps will also help you identify any phrases you have missed.

TOP TIP 39 Try a pay-per-click (PPC) advertising programme.

Google Adwords, MSN Adcenter and Yahoo! Search Marketing are the best-known schemes. PPC ads can be useful and cost-effective traffic generators in their own right, and you should at least test them. But they attract fewer clicks than natural or 'organic' listings and are generally much more expensive than optimizing your site for those. However, you can get a "double whammy" by using PPC as you both test whether PPC is cost-effective and also test out how good various key words are. You can subsequently optimize for the natural listings using the best-performing key phrases.

TOP TIP 40 Include the key phrases early in the title tag.

For example, suppose you are running a sailing site and you have decided that 'boats for sale' and 'yachts for sale' are the search phrases your potential customers are most likely to use. You would set up your tags something like this:

<HEAD>
<TITLE>Boats for sale and yachts for sale from Seven Seas Sailing</TITLE>
<META Name='description' Content='boats for sale, yachts for sale and everything you need to know about sailing'>
<META Name='keywords' Content='boats for sale yachts for sale sailing sails">
</HEAD>

TOP TIP **41** Repeat the key phrases at least four times near the top of your web page.

If your page is based on a table, this will mean placing them near the top of the left-hand column. Add a Meta Description tag (as shown in the previous tip), but don't worry about Meta Keywords tags unless you know you will be targeting a search engine that uses them. Most don't. Also, work your key phrases into text that describes your site, so it reads well for visitors.

TOP TIP **42** Get as many links to your pages as possible from other relevant sites.

This will affect your ranking in some major search engines. The text of the link should ideally include one or more of your key phrases.

TOP TIP **43** Act natural.

Don't try to conceal key phrases, for example by putting them in small or white text or in the same colour as the background. And don't 'spam' by repeating key phrases mindlessly. You may be blacklisted irrevocably by the search engines for using these kind of tricks.

TOP TIP **44** Don't use frames.

It complicates things. In some cases, search engines will not link through them. However well your pages are optimised, they won't get ranked if the search engines can only find the frameset page. In other cases, the search engines will drive visitors straight to the content frames, missing out the frameset page, and customers will not be able to navigate elsewhere within the site.

45 Manually submit your pages to your target search engines.

Make sure you include the major search providers listed below (note some require payment). Don't worry about the hundreds of others, and don't believe any pitch that emphasises them.

The key ones are:

Google

Yahoo! (web sites and directory)

MSN

Open Directory (dmoz.org)

46 Consider concentrating on smaller search engines.

If you operate in a market where there is a lot of traffic through search engines and a lot of competition, consider concentrating your effort on smaller search engines. You may get better results for the same expenditure, and the overall market volume means that there are still good pickings, even from the smallest engines.

47 Avoid the scam where a supplier offers you "guaranteed top rankings".

No-one can guarantee top rankings except for phrases that aren't important and will generate hardly any traffic. So that's what you will get.

Marketing your website:

Top tips for turning browsers into buyers

Selling successfully to people who browse on the internet has many of the elements of ordinary sales and marketing, but there are some subtle differences. For a start, the demographics of people who shop on the web can be different from those who shop in the high street, unless you happen to be selling hi-tech equipment or gadgets. Then there are the limitations of the medium. The internet is good for products where you can make a judgement based upon sight or sound, but less good where smell, taste or touch matter. If you need more than sight or sound then you will have to build trust - customers will need to have confidence that fruit will be ripe, clothes will fit and so on. You can build trust by establishing a reputation, and by reducing the risk to the buyer by offering a truly no-quibble returns policy.

The key to sales is offering what the customer wants, at a price they are happy to pay. In your e-store, the buyer cannot easily ask questions of you, so you need to provide all the information they require to make a decision. It is very easy to drive someone away on the web - the world is only a click away - so minimize the barriers to buying. Remember, once they have arrived at your web site, the marketing has finished and the selling begins.

TOP TIP **48** Do not ask them to log in or supply any
details before they can look at your products.

There will be plenty of time to get their name and address once
they have decided to buy something. It is nice to offer regular customers
some form of recognition, like showing their name, but if you ask for it
too early, it's like an over-familiar salesman. Most buyers will leave your
site rather than fill in a form. Your job is to eliminate everything that gets
in the way of making a sale.

TOP TIP **49** Do not use Flash, large images,
front doors or other gimmicks.

If you really need a short introduction, then at least have the
grace to offer a 'Skip intro' link. Otherwise, 80-90% of your visitors will
leave without opening the door. The rest will watch the animation and
then leave. Ask yourself - do I need to impress, or to sell something?

TOP TIP **50** Do make it easy to find your
products and services.

If you have a home page, have a clear link such as 'Shop Here' in
large letters. Do not rely on clever graphics or animations. Do not make
it flash or blink - everyone will assume that the rest of the site will give
them migraines! Even better, use your home page as part of the store
and start selling straight away.

TOP TIP **51** Make it easy to recognise
what it is that you sell.

Have pictures of the sort of products that you sell in each
category - some of your buyers may not speak your language, but they
know what they want to buy. If you sell branded goods, use the brand
logos (get permission) to reinforce your credibility and to speed people
through. Link logos to the relevant sales section.

TOP TIP 52 Keep it simple.

Make sure it is obvious how to add something to the shopping basket, and use common metaphors. If they cannot see how to buy, they won't - there is always another store to go to.

TOP TIP 53 Provide good searching.

Make sure that searching is fast and accurate, and provide attribute-based searches as well as keywords. Create a drop-down list of the common attributes of your products to supplement your normal keyword searching. If someone is looking for a four-door car on your site, they don't want to have to guess if you called it 'four-door', '4-door', '4dr' or something else.

TOP TIP 54 Keep your site up to date.

If you have goods that go out of stock, take them off the site or mark them as 'temporarily out of stock'. Make sure that your terms and conditions explain what happens if items do run out of stock. The internet is very good for disposing of 'dead stock' at discount prices, but keep this in a separate section from your regular items so that you can update it easily. And if you have any fixed-term offers, take them down as soon as they have expired.

TOP TIP 55 Have special prices and your fastest moving goods on your entry page.

Nothing succeeds like success. You need to grab customers and start taking their orders at the earliest possible point. Your top sellers and best offers will always have the greatest appeal.

TOP TIP **56** Offer to keep the name and address of buyers - you can use a cookie on their browser to avoid security issues.

This will allow your customers to checkout without having to type all their details in again. They will appreciate it, and it's an incentive to shop again. But do make it clear that a cookie is being used, and give them the option not to store it - after all, they might be in an internet café.

TOP TIP **57** Make your promises and guarantees clear and unequivocal.

Include them within the checkout process, even if they appear elsewhere on the web site. You need to inspire confidence in buyers who have never met you. If you ever have an issue, just make the refund - unhappy customers tell many more people than happy ones do, and will also waste lots of your time.

TOP TIP **58** Provide the most comprehensive information on your products that you can.

Nothing is more off-putting than not knowing what you are buying or not being sure if it will work the way that you need it to. For instance, will it work with your 24 volt system? If you don't supply the information, your prospect will click away to someone who does.

TOP TIP **59** If possible, provide ways that customers can ask for more information.

Make sure that you respond in a timely manner. For instance, you might encourage them to email you questions. Alternatively, you might provide a telephone hotline, or enable an instant messaging service so that they can chat in real time while looking at your store.

Marketing your website:

Top tips to avoid abandoned shopping carts

Abandoned shopping carts aren't necessarily negative. Visitors quit their carts for many reasons. They may be competitors checking out your site, or consumers comparing prices and finding out your trading policies. Equally, customers may use your site and then place the order by telephone.

On the other hand, shoppers may quit because they find your checkout too complicated, or because they can't find a next-day delivery option. The following tips will help you minimize unnecessary abandonment, and encourage consumers to complete their purchase and to buy again.

TOP TIP **60** Most importantly, build trust and more trust.

Provide your contact details throughout the site, including a telephone number and physical address. Promote confidence, respond quickly to emails, and answer the telephone professionally.

TOP TIP **61** Keep your site simple and easy to use.

Divide the site into logical sections, with clear navigation links and a link to the home page on every page of the site. Give full information with each product. Provide a search facility. And make sure that customers can get from home page to 'Buy now' button in the minimum number of mouse clicks.

TOP TIP
62 Communicate your shipping costs early in the transaction.

Everyone hates surprises on cost. If the customer proceeds to checkout and decides the postage is too expensive, you have lost the sale. However, to justify a single postage charge, a customer may buy more than one product.

TOP TIP
63 Explain your guarantee and returns policy.

A rock solid guarantee goes a long way to persuading people to buy.

TOP TIP
64 Describe your terms and conditions.

When people can't find information, they tend to assume the worst. Go out of your way to provide comprehensive buyer friendly information, and your privacy policy. Make your site one that you would like to buy from.

TOP TIP
65 Explain your security and encryption process.

Offer customers the visible security of the 'golden padlock' that comes with using a Secure Socket Layer (SSL) on your site. Your ISP or web host can advise you how to set this up - or you can use a secure payment service like the one offered by Actinic.

TOP TIP
66 Categorise your site content into attractors (what people like) and detractors.

Try to minimize detractors (ad pop-ups, need to register before buying and so on) and at worst balance them with attractors.

TOP TIP

67 Experiment.

Different site layouts and options can have a dramatic and unexpected impact on sales. For instance, one site reported a 20% increase in revenue after they added Paypal as a payment option. Another reported a 50% reduction after they prominently added the ability to input a voucher during checkout. People who did not have vouchers were obviously put off. Experimenting is important because each site will have slightly different visitor demographics - meaning that the people who visit different sites will behave differently. So you need to do your own trials.

TOP TIP

68 Remember customer service is key.

Encourage repeat business by going out of your way to meet customer needs. A happy customer will tell his friends, but an unhappy one will tell anybody who will listen.

TOP TIP

69 Be available.

If customers cannot find out what they want to know from your site, they may try to get in touch with you. If they are unsuccessful, they will expect the same difficulty if they ever have a problem with an order - and they will go elsewhere.

Marketing your website:

Top tips for pricing and promotion

TOP TIP **70** Always offer more for slightly more money.
Never discount something that a lot of people will buy anyway, it will cost you much more. Offer them a great deal if they buy something else at the same time. This will please them and encourage them to come back, and it will increase the value of each sale that you make.

TOP TIP **71** Provide the ability to buy associated products.
Encourage customers to purchase batteries with battery powered equipment, paper and toner with printers and so on. They have to buy those things from someone. If you make it easy to buy them all together, they are more likely to buy them from you.

TOP TIP **72** Use vouchers or coupons.
A person with a voucher or coupon feels that they have a special deal. It also ties them in to buying from you, because they cannot redeem your vouchers anywhere else.

TOP TIP **73** Email electronic coupons.

That way they are exclusive to your email group, and you reward your loyal customers without losing out on potential revenue from one-time buyers.

TOP TIP **74** Understand how customers behave in your market.

That will determine which tactics will work. Watch the trends in pricing and promotions among your competitors and in related markets. Learn from them, try things out, and see what works.

TOP TIP **75** Try to find ways of reducing price for those who are very price conscious, at a cost to them.

Airlines do this by discounting seats booked way in advance and sometimes at the very last minute, both of which are less convenient and popular than booking a few weeks in advance. You might do this by discounting returned goods or end-of-lines. Provided that it's not loss making, it's better to sell to price conscious customers at a discount than to lose the business to the competition.

TOP TIP **76** Get customers to return
to your online store.

Analyse their sales patterns and make a special offer if they
haven't come for a while. Get and retain their permission to keep in
touch with them by email by making it worth their while.

TOP TIP **77** If you make a special offer,
make sure that it really is special.

Have you been put off by companies that say something is
special, but it's hardly worth having? Or by offers made under a "loyalty
scheme" - and badged as such - that turn out to be the same as offers
being made to everyone else?

TOP TIP **78** Analyse the value of your
offering to customers.

Make sure the actual value (to a business) or perceived value
(to consumers) exceeds what you will charge them. Otherwise you will
always be trying to sweep water uphill.

TOP TIP **79** Don't under-price.

The quickest way that you can destroy a business is to engage
in a price war where no-one makes any money. Make your offering the
best overall value, not necessarily the cheapest - unless you have clear
cost advantages which mean that you can sell low and still make a
good profit.

80 Upsell in your cart and after they have ordered.

Once people have placed items in the cart, offer further items at a discount. You could offer the extra items post-free as an incentive; you may want to identify your best selling lines, or to look at linkages between items (e.g. batteries with toys or a case with a laptop). With good software, you can do this easily. A customer who has just decided to buy is generally feeling favourable towards you - so it's an ideal time to sell them something else. You could contact the customer post-sale to check everything is OK and to suggest some more possibilities.

This gives a personal touch to your operation as well as generating additional revenue.

Security and the law

Security and the law:

Top tips to convince visitors transactions are safe

Once upon a time, customers needed convincing that the internet was a safe place to shop. Internet novices still need that reassurance. But most people nowadays have shopped online at least once. They take it for granted that buying online is safe - but they still need to be persuaded that it's safe to buy from you. Here are some tips for convincing both groups.

Whether you deliver electronically or by carrier pigeon you face the same initial challenge. You need to establish trust. Customers cannot look around your premises to see how you store goods, how much dust is on them or whether your staff play frisbee with CDs. In a physical store, they can chat to the owner and look around. If they can see what they want on a shelf then they know it's in stock and in reasonable condition. You have to try to achieve the same confidence from your buyers.

TOP TIP **81** Reassure visitors that you are real.

As a vendor, you should list your actual address and phone number, and provide a point of contact where your web site visitors can speak to a real person. Also, if applicable provide your company registration and VAT numbers as it is the law to do so. Say on the site: 'If you have any questions or queries about us or our products, please call us'. Provide facts about your business, and maybe pictures, as this will promote confidence. This point has been repeated from earlier. Deliberately. It's that important.

TOP TIP

82 Join a professional scheme.

These provide reassurance for shoppers through a system of independent registration and verification of online retailers. SafeBuy or the IMRG's Internet Shopping is Safe (ISIS) scheme are the best known. Display the logo on your home page, but not in the checkout. You don't want people to stop and think twice about security when they are about to make a purchase.

TOP TIP

83 Credit card companies protect buyers.

Many people don't realize the extent of protection that their credit card companies provide. It's simple. If you get transactions charged to your account which you didn't authorize, you can request a refund from your credit card issuer. So let them know.

TOP TIP

84 Buying online is as safe as buying by mail order.

Risks on the internet are the same as in mail order. If you feel confident to purchase by phone, fax or mail, you should be confident to buy on the internet. In fact, your rights are the same whether shopping on the net or in the high street. In the EU they are covered by the Distance Selling Directive; in the UK, by the Sale of Goods Act 1979 and the Trade Descriptions Act 1976 as well. If you receive faulty goods you have the right to a full refund. The only exception is when buying from abroad.

TOP TIP

85 Buying online is no riskier than many personal transactions.

The risk is actually no greater than using your card in other places. For instance, when you use your card in a restaurant, all of the information that you make available online can be seen by the waiter. And as the new security systems "Verified by Visa" and "Mastercard Secure" roll out, the risk will probably be lower for online buyers than for others.

TOP TIP **86** Encryption is the key.

Credit card information is fully encrypted by virtually all vendors as it travels over the net. Provide details of your security method. This usually comes from using Secure Socket Layer (SSL).

TOP TIP **87** All of the big boys do it.

Billions of pounds of transactions are now being conducted across the internet every month. This is despite viruses and all of the other problems. Thousands and thousands of purchases are taking place, and many huge companies such as Dell are making the web their main ordering mechanism. Would they do this if it was fundamentally insecure?

TOP TIP **88** Offer alternative ordering and payment methods.

As a vendor, even if you are pushing web sales hard you should give alternative ways of ordering such as by fax. A few people will take advantage of the facility, but for the rest it shows that you are fully confident. And offer additional methods of payment such as cheque or PayPal.

TOP TIP **89** Use your existing credentials.

If you are a member of a professional body, display their logo prominently on your home page - provided this is permitted under your terms of membership.

TOP TIP 90 Present customer endorsements.

Whenever customers make positive comments about your company, try to get their permission to quote them on your web site. Scatter a few such endorsements around the site, and change them regularly.

TOP TIP 91 Put some pictures of staff and your premises if you can.

It helps to establish how real you are, and is much more appealing than a faceless organisation.

Security and the law:

Top tips to be legal and decent

Like every area of business these days, ecommerce is surrounded by a maze of red tape, rules and regulations. In fact, selling online tends to be worse because of the international dimension. And any slip-ups you make are there for the world to see - so it's doubly important to be legal and decent. These tips try to pull together some of the areas that you need to think about and understand. They shouldn't be taken as definitive - it's your responsibility to comply with the law - but they are a good place to start.

TOP TIP **92** Get your VAT registration right.
You must be VAT registered if your annual sales exceed the current VAT threshold, which changes every year but is around £64,000 (Search on Google UK for "vat registration threshold" to get the most up-to-date figure). If you're not VAT registered, you don't have to worry about charging VAT and it would actually be against the law to do so.

TOP TIP **93** Understand tax on shipping.
People often don't understand the finer points of VAT. For instance, if your products are a mixture of VATable and non-VATable, then the VAT charged on shipping should be in proportion to the mixture of VATable and non-VATable goods. Make sure your ecommerce solution can handle all of the VAT rules.

TOP TIP **94** Exempt EU business buyers from tax.

If your customer is a non-UK business in the EU and is registered for VAT in their own country, they are allowed to quote their VAT registration number to you in order to be exempted from tax. If you can't accommodate this, those customers are likely to look elsewhere.

TOP TIP **95** Charge the country VAT rate if you exceed the country VAT threshold.

Not many people know this, but if your online store is wildly successful and you are starting to turn over serious bucks selling into other EU countries, you hit some additional regulations. If you exceed the individual VAT threshold for Germany, France, etc. then you should charge VAT at the appropriate country VAT rate when selling into that country, not the usual UK 17.5% rate.

TOP TIP **96** Remember your jurisdiction.

We're in the EU so we are bound by EU rules. It's not the same when handling US buyers. US states might want to charge tax on sales into their area, but it's their responsibility to levy this tax. You don't have to charge this "use tax" which is between the buyer and the state where they live. So as a UK business you can sell into the US tax free.

TOP TIP **97** Comply with the EU distance selling directive.

Under the EU Distance Selling Directive, you must make clear who you are by providing full contact details including an address and phone number. This is also good practice for building trust.

TOP TIP **98** Offer a 7 day return option.

Also under the EU Distance Selling Directive, you must accept goods for return within 7 working days. Why not make this a selling point?

TOP TIP **99** Allow for disabled visitors - it's the law.

Make sure that you comply with the disability discrimination law. The key requirement is that you have to take "reasonable" steps to provide access to people with disabilities, and this includes your online store. One way of doing that is to make sure that all images have alternate ('Alt') text tags so visually impaired people can still navigate your site.

TOP TIP **100** Privacy matters.

You probably need to register with the Data Protection Registry at www.dpr.gov.uk. Registering takes just a few hours of careful work and thought.

TOP TIP **101** Comply with the rules on sending email.

The law about emailing is somewhat ambiguous. The generally accepted rule of thumb is that you can email anyone who gave you their address in the course of making a purchase or enquiring about a product; but every email you send must include an 'unsubscribe' option to enable recipients to opt out of future mailings. In the case of bought in lists, the addressees must have explicitly agreed to receive emails from a third party. Best practice is to provide several options, and allow individuals to specify what type of communications they would like to receive from you.

TOP TIP **102** In conclusion, turn these burdens into benefits.

Assuming that you are legal and decent, let the world know. Anything that adds to your credibility will help online. So why not list all of the things that you have done under the heading "We comply with the following legal and tax regulations"?

Shipping

Shipping:

Considerations for shipping and distribution

People who buy in a hurry expect the goods to be delivered in a hurry too. This is no problem for digital products like music, software and images where delivery can be made electronically. It's harder when you have physical goods to be shipped to the customer. Distribution is an area where bricks and mortar companies may even have an edge. If you already have a warehouse and make mail-order sales, then you are better placed than a startup company that only has a web site.

As a merchant, you need to be clear with your customers what you offer and then live by it. If you outsource, be aware that you can't outsource responsibility. Buyers don't care why you have failed or whose fault it is - all they care about is getting what they have paid for. So here are ten tips for making a success of your distribution.

TOP TIP **103** Manage customer expectations.

In an e-store you need to make sure that customers know exactly what they will get, and when. Amazon tell you that a book 'normally ships in 2-3 days' so you aren't too upset if it takes four. If you offer '24 hour delivery' then when do the 24 hours start? What are the time constraints, e.g. 'Orders received by 4pm normally ship the same day'.

TOP TIP **104** No surprises for the customer.

Make sure that you calculate shipping charges as part of the whole deal. You may need to charge by weight, by volume or by value of order. If you offer free shipping on orders over a certain value, make it clear whether that value includes tax.

TOP TIP **105** Living with back orders.

Back orders are a fact of life if you accept fax or mail-orders, so expect them in internet selling too. Allow the buyer the choice of waiting for a complete shipment or taking part orders. Only charge shipping once - it is irritating being charged extra shipping when it is the merchant's fault that the item was not in stock. If this can't work economically, cancel back orders and inform the customer. Make it clear on the site how you will deal with these sorts of situations.

TOP TIP **106** Give plenty of feedback.

Placing an internet order may feel risky for the buyer. Make sure your buyers are told that you have received their order, and keep them up to date with its progress. If you have to make a back-order, let the buyer know when the rest of the order is expected.

TOP TIP **107** Pick a reliable carrier.

There are lots of carriers and they compete heavily. Value reliability over price. A lost buyer will probably cost you more than the difference in shipping cost. Pick a carrier that can track goods online. Give the tracking reference to your customer as part of the order processing feedback. Monitor the performance of your carriers.

TOP TIP **108** Be clear about returns and guarantees.

Sadly, some of your sales will come back to you. Some may be your fault but others may be beyond your control. Publish your returns policy and include it as part of the ordering process at the web site. Be clear about who will pay for return carriage. If it is you then make sure your carrier can collect.

TOP TIP **109** Say what you mean and mean what you say.

Don't over-promise. Repeat customers are much more valuable than one-offs. Make it clear when you will deliver and then stick to it - even if it costs you more. Customers appreciate merchants who go out of their way to meet their commitments.

TOP TIP **110** Selling overseas.

There are all sorts of pitfalls to exporting. Who is responsible for any duty or taxes on the goods? In Europe, the EU Directive on Distance Selling sets out a legal framework for shipping within the EU. The good news is that shipments within the EU are free of duty. In the US, Congress banned new internet taxes - but government policy can change. Most large carriers can collect duty on goods when they arrive, but you need to be clear about who is going to pick up the tab. Generally it is the buyer's responsibility. Make sure they know. If it comes as a surprise to them when the goods are delivered, you are the one they will blame.

TOP TIP **111** Will your customer be in when it arrives?

Customers usually have to go to work, so there may be problems in receiving your goods. One obvious solution is to deliver to workplaces, or allow special delivery instructions like "deliver to neighbour at number 5". Some companies are experimenting with deliveries to known drop-off points like petrol service stations. If you can offer this, make sure that you can deal with goods that 'go missing' en-route. Another approach is to offer delivery within more precise time periods.

TOP TIP **112** Can you outsource it all?

Outsourcing fulfillment can be attractive - letting a warehousing company store and ship the goods. Make sure it is clear who bears the risk of stock in the warehouse, both for fire and theft. If the warehouse contents vanish, who is left with the bill? If rats nibble your books, who pays? Check that you are properly insured if it's your risk. Insure it anyway if it's theirs - who knows if they have paid their premiums? Check on their performance - it is your reputation at stake.

Customer relationship management

Customer relationship management:

Ways to show customers you care

It's one thing to present a great appearance to a new customer and win their first order. Now you have to deliver the service you have led them to expect! If you can demonstrate that you really look after your customers and give them a great experience, they are very likely to come back and order again and again. The simple key to showing customers you care is to ask what you would like if you were a customer.

TOP TIP **113** Don't talk about it, do it.

If there's anything worse than bad service, it's receiving bad service after you've been told how great the service is. It's much better to actually provide good service than deliver platitudes about it.

TOP TIP **114** Once they have placed an order with you, send an immediate acknowledgement that you have received it.

This can be automated by your ecommerce package or you may choose to send a personal note. It is much easier for small companies to offer such personal touches than for corporates with their larger volume of orders.

TOP TIP **115** Keep the customer informed.

If you can afford it, pro-actively monitor deliveries. Find out from your carriers what didn't get delivered as promised, then contact your customer to let them know what's happening. Customers will think this is great service, and it turns a failure into a demonstration that you care.

TOP TIP **116** Go multi-channel.

If you have a printed catalog, ask if they would like a copy when they order. Don't feel that the web is your only channel - you have multiple routes to your customer. It is much easier and cheaper to sell more to an existing customer than it is to win a new one. Research suggests that customers who buy through multiple channels are the most profitable customers.

TOP TIP **117** Look for every opportunity to personalise your service.

The internet is generally very impersonal, so you need to communicate that your business is run by human beings who care about their customers. This also reassures them that they have a contact, if there is any problem - it is much better than a faceless corporation.

TOP TIP **118** Image is an issue when a customer has never met you.

Take all the chances you have to exceed expectations and build your reputation. If you need to call a customer for any reason - for example for security purposes, if the credit card and delivery addresses are different - take the opportunity to offer something extra such as a gift-wrap service. This helps protect you without offending the customer.

TOP TIP **119** If there are any problems, like out of stock items or a problem with delivery, tell the customer immediately and take full responsibility.

Never, ever blame anyone else - even the courier. Nothing is more infuriating for the consumer than when a supplier blames some third-party over whom they have no control.

TOP TIP **120** When a mistake happens, correct it at the highest level.

Customers appreciate it when a manager calls, rather than the most junior person - it makes them feel important to the company. Also the manager has more power to offer compensation or to rectify the problem. An apology works wonders, especially if it is accompanied by a token to acknowledge the problem, such as a discount voucher against future orders.

TOP TIP **121** Review your service continually.

Contact customers, or a cross section of customers, some time after delivery and check that they are happy with what they bought and with your service to them. You can do this by email or by telephone. This gives you feedback on your operation and also gives you another legitimate chance to sell something. Your customer may have ordered one of something to try it out - if they are happy, you may get a larger order immediately. If they have any problems, apologise and deal with them.

TOP TIP **122** Remind everyone in your organization that you are one company.

It is everyone's problem if a customer is unhappy. Never let one department or staff member criticise another; customers will not be reassured about a company that is warring with itself. Focus on beating your competitors, not your colleagues.

TOP TIP **123** Treat customer complaints as an opportunity, not a problem.

As well as exposing specific problems that need to be fixed, customer complaints are a great opportunity to learn and improve. They should not be buried away and forgotten, but analysed. It's also good to share both positive and negative feedback with everyone in the organization. If staff are mentioned by name, pass this on for praise but don't publish it in the case of criticism. This reminds everyone how important it is to keep customers happy - and provides a well-earned pat on the back when things go well.

Last thoughts

Last thoughts

We don't want to miss anything out so here are some additional tips on a variety of topics.

TOP TIP **124** Avoid fraud.

One problem when selling online is fraud. Don't get things out of proportion, there are problems with any business and no-one has managed to entirely eliminate shoplifting yet. Unfortunately it's true that foreign orders from some countries seem to be much more likely to be fraudulent than others. If in doubt, stick to ones from Western Europe and North America. To help avoid fraudulent orders look out for these indicators of fraud:

• They tend to use the most expensive shipping method available
• They tend to choose the most expensive products
• They tend to use free email addresses such as Yahoo or Hotmail.

In addition you can check whether an order is fraudulent by asking for a fax of a copy of the back strip of the credit card; asking for proof of name and address to be faxed; or you can telephone to make sure that the number is genuine. Most fraudsters give up at the first hurdle and you don't hear from them again. If you use a payment service such as Actinic or Worldpay, this normally provides some standard anti-fraud measures.

TOP TIP **125** If you can't get big, get niche.

The world wide web is huge, but you can be successful by being different. Maybe you can present a range of specialist products that is hard to find elsewhere.

TOP TIP **126** Be realistic.

Not everything can be sold online. If you can't buy it by telephone, it probably won't sell over the net. But it is surprising just what does work.

TOP TIP **127** Choose a solution that can grow with your business.

Remember - you get what you pay for. Choose proven software with proper security that is capable of handling your business growth. Make sure that the supplier is successful enough to still be around in a few years' time.

Thank you for getting this far.

That's it! It just remains for us to wish you success with your online venture. We hope that you join the ranks of those making a decent living from the web, or even become one of the elite making a genuine fortune.

About Actinic

Since 1996, Actinic has been helping small and medium businesses trade online easily and at low cost. Actinic is a leading supplier of packaged ecommerce and EPOS solutions for retailers, and ecommerce development software for web designers.

Actinic provides award-winning applications that include everything a small or medium business needs to build and and manage their online or bricks and mortar store. All products integrate every element of an online store into a single turnkey solution, from site design and maintenance through to processing of orders and printing of invoices. Site design can be customized from a range of design theme templates, and catalogue updates are easy to make. A built-in order processing facility includes support for phone, fax and mail orders; flexible shipping and tax handling; back-ordering; stock monitoring; and reporting. Actinic integrates with all leading payment providers.

The Actinic range embraces options priced and capable of supporting businesses from part-time start-ups through to hundreds of thousands of orders and tens of millions of pounds per annum.

For more information and a FREE 30-day trial, visit www.actinic.co.uk/tt
Trademarks are acknowledged.